Plainsongs

Editor

Eric R. Tucker

Associate Editors

Becky Faber, Michael Catherwood, Eleanor Reeds

Publisher

Corpus Callosum Press

Corpus Callosum Press

Hastings, Nebraska

Subscriptions to *Plainsongs* are $25.00 annually for two issues, published in January and July. Subscriptions can be purchased online at the Corpus Callosum Press website.

Plainsongs welcomes submissions. The manuscript deadline for the Winter 2022 issue is June 15, 2021. Contributors will receive one free copy of the issue in which their poem appears. For each issue, the Board of Readers will select three poems to be honored as award poems. Award poem winners will receive a small monetary amount, currently $50.

Please use our online submission manager, available on the Corpus Callosum Press website, to submit work. We cannot guarantee responses for work submitted through any other method. For more information about submitting poetry or subscribing to *Plainsongs*, please see our new website: https://www.corpuscallosumpress.com/plainsongs.

Front and back cover photos by B.T.W.

Plainsongs is indexed by Humanities International Complete, EBSCO Information Services, 10 Estes Street, Ipswich, MA 01938.

ISBN-13 978-0-9996869-6-6

ISSN 1534-3820

Plainsongs

Winner of the Jane Geske Award,
presented by the Nebraska Center for the Book

Notes from the Editor

I'm pretty sure I've never written or uttered the words *will usher in* in that particular order. I think I would know if I had; it just seems like something I'd remember. I do recall the first time I said the word *salutary*, and to this day I'm not sure if I pronounced it properly. The start of a new year would appear to present a primo opportunity to finally scratch that long-standing *will usher in* itch. But right now, during a particularly dismal phase of the pandemic, when the numbers of infections and deaths are horrifically high, and with widespread vaccine distribution likely not happening until summer at the earliest, the thought of writing about anything ushering anyone into anywhere feels linguistically irresponsible.

But the year 2021 can, and will, *inaugurate*, thank goodness. It will start, it will commence, it will kick off. Change is afoot in 2021; perhaps one can find some hope in that. The prolonged bleakness of 2020 brings to mind a different kind of usher. In Poe's famous gothic short story, the narrator flees the Usher family mansion and its suffocating atmosphere of dread and paranoia just before the house splits in two and sinks into a lake; our escape from 2020 feels similarly fraught and skin-of-our-teeth fortuitous. Another childhood home haunted by painful memories is described by poet Zachary Schomburg in his surreal poem "Scary, No Scary": "The old man / hunched over / at the front door / will be prepared / to give you a tour, / but first he'll ask / *Scary, or no scary?* // You should say / *No scary*."

A profound change, simultaneously scary and no scary, has occurred here at *Plainsongs*: the journal is now published by Corpus Callosum Press, a small literary press based in Hastings, Nebraska. We are grateful to Hastings College and particularly Dr. Patricia Oman at HC Press for providing *Plainsongs* with a loving and supportive home for so many years. And we are excited to see *Plainsongs* continue to flourish under the banner of Corpus Callosum Press.

We hope you enjoy this issue, which features award poems by Hayden Saunier, Laura Saint Martin, and John Matthew Steinhafel, with accompanying essays by associate editors Becky Faber, Eleanor Reeds, and Michael Catherwood. One thing that will never change at *Plainsongs* is our gratitude for your continued support. We hope 2021 kicks off a period for you that is safe, salutary, and no scary.

Eric R. Tucker
Hastings, Nebraska

Contents

Men Walking on the Moon, 50th Anniversary 10
    Hayden Saunier
About "Men Walking on the Moon, 50th Anniversary":
A *Plainsongs* Award Poem 11
    Becky Faber
Cattywampus 12
    Laura Saint Martin
About "Cattywampus": A *Plainsongs* Award Poem 13
    Eleanor Reeds
My Neighbor Henry 14
    John Matthew Steinhafel
About "My Neighbor Henry": A *Plainsongs* Award Poem 16
    Michael Catherwood
Persimmons 17
    Jayne Macke
Seduction at the Oregon Coast Aquarium 18
    Shelley Reece
Biopsy 19
    Peter Snow
He's losing words 20
    Rose Mary Boehm
Cheerfully 21
    P M F Johnson
Anemone 22
    Daniel E. Blackston
Houseflies 23
    Faiz Ahmad
Hard Winter 24
    Kathy Jacobs
A Tipsy Librarian 26
    Mickie Kennedy
Some Winter 27
    Jane Costain
The Itch 28
    Emily Hockaday
Living with Hawks 29
    Elisabeth Harrahy
Hitchhiking at 19 30
    Jo-Anne Cappeluti
Thoreau Reconsiders 31
    Ken Craft
Orbit of Tongues 32
    Gwenn Nusbaum
The Percipient 33
    Harry Moore
Self-Portrait in Mixed Media 34
    Trisha Daigle

night ode 35
   Ali Beheler
The Secret 36
   Marilyn Dorf
Suicide Watch 37
   B.J. Wilson
High Wire Suite 38
   Lee Peterson
social distancing 40
   Doritt Carroll
Midafternoon, December 41
   Lisa Roullard
Better Embers 42
   Thomas Mixon
Midwest Crossing 43
   Kathryn Paulsen
Undone 44
   Yvonne Nguyen
Learning Long Division 45
   George Rawlins
A Friend Tells Me an Anecdote about What It's Like to Be Black in America 46
   Michael DeMaranville
Mermaids in the Basement 48
   Shirley J. Brewer
Mama's Suffering 49
   Brittany J. Barron
Gutestellezumhalten…or is it *Zumhaltengezwungenerort* 50
   Renée Adams
Digital Happy Hour 51
   Timothy McNeil Grant
This Is Not That Poem 52
   Tom Barlow
The River 53
   Larry Smith
Jackson County Pantoum 54
   Nolan Meditz
Four Seasons 55
   Gloria Heffernan
meeresstille 56
   Maggie Wang
The Old Apple Tree 57
   Mark Rhoads
Fishing for a Reader 58
   Ryan Nelson
To the God Living in My Last Alveoli 59
   Marc Tretin
You Visit Me in a Dream at 3:36 AM 60
   Callie S. Blackstone
Face in Her Phone 61
   Bonnie Larson Staiger

Open Casket 62
    Brittany Smart
Pink Plastic Caboodle 63
    Stephanie Valente
Spoken Over 64
    Emily Uduwana
Because Memory Is Not Linear 65
    Bethany Reid
Silver Screen 66
    Michael Hill
It's Always within the Wood 67
    Jack Ridl
Yes, No, Yes: An Acrostic 68
    Amy Spungen
The Scent of Rain 69
    Beth Paulson
Some Marriage Vows 70
    William Greene
Perhaps Then 71
    Stephanie Lamb
Ides of March 72
    Peter Neil Carroll
Indigo Barn on the Way to the Reading 74
    Suzanne Swanson
The Sleeping Princess 76
    Hailey Spencer
Burn 77
    Ann Schlotzhauer
How we remember and how we forget 78
    Susan Harvey
Breathe 79
    Barbara Tramonte
Grappling with a Bit of Astrophysics and the Optimum Wrinkle Cream 80
    Frank H. Coons
Prelude to Pandemic 81
    Abby Caplin
Dear God of Condiments 82
    Gray Thomas
Hegel's Head 83
    Bruce Alford
Anatomous 84
    Casey Killingsworth
Rose in a Blue Vase 85
    Kathleen McCann
Include Everyone 86
    Cassie Premo Steele
The Streetsweeper 87
    Cameron Morse
Core 88
    Bill Griffin

Letter to an Imaginary Friend	89
Saramanda Swigart	
Blue Crayon	90
Richard T. Rauch	
Muddy Water	92
Ruth Holzer	
Another Poem about Birds and Windows	93
Katie Tunning	
Dead Poets Society	94
Jade Driscoll	
Gonna Tell My Kids	95
Gretchen Gales	
Earth Wrapped Wood	96
Haley Wooning	
Unencumbered	97
Robert L. Penick	
Marx and Bakunin	98
Jones Irwin	
With My Mother on the Patio	99
Jae Dyche	
We Need Your Help	100
Michelle Brooks	
Cheesecake Monument	101
Kelly Hegi	
Downhill	102
Stephen Ground	
Every Body Lies	103
AE Hines	
Preparing for Our Past	104
Bradley David	
After	106
Margaret Adams Birth	
She wears a larch collar	107
Ed Sage	
Encounters with Strangers II	108
Joseph Felkers	
comfort	110
Benjamin Mast	
Chokecherry	111
Austin Veldman	
Sassafras Tree in Snow	112
Stuart Gunter	

Men Walking on the Moon, 50th Anniversary

We were all remembering where
we'd been that night, and if alive, how young

we were, when a friend said it was the only time
she ever heard her father talk about the war

he'd fought in years before in the Pacific.
That when he saw the first footprints

deep in lunar dust—how the boots had stamped
themselves down into the soft white surface

and no wind stirred—he said: that's what
the ground was like at Nagasaki when we

were sent in afterward. Our boot prints sunk
into ash. Then he said nothing more.

Hayden Saunier
Bedminster, Pennsylvania

About "Men Walking on the Moon, 50th Anniversary": A *Plainsongs* Award Poem

"Men Walking on the Moon, 50th Anniversary" drew me in right away; I remember where I was that night and how it felt to look up at the moon to imagine humans on its surface. [For those needing historical context, Neil Armstrong walked on the moon on July 20, 1969; the U.S. dropped an atomic bomb on Nagasaki, Japan, on August 9, 1945.]

I wasn't prepared for where the poem was headed—how the poet would move from moon dust to atomic dust. The two-line stanzas provide smooth flow, thus making an effortless transition from the moon walk to the soldier entering Nagasaki after the bomb. The comparison of the lunar surface to the "lunar dust" where "the boots had stamped/themselves down into the soft white surface" is striking.

Equally effective is the shift in pronouns. The poem begins with the "we" of friends discussing their memories of July 20, 1969. "We" becomes "she," then "he" as one of the group moves the focus to her father's description of entering Nagasaki twenty-four years earlier. The pronoun shifts back to first-person plural: "that's what / the ground was like at Nagasaki when we / were sent in afterward. Our boot prints sunk / into ash." In such a short poem, movements of this kind can be confusing, but here it is well crafted.

In the last few years I've written about veterans and their military experiences. I've had a number of conversations with their relatives who often say that the veteran NEVER talks about his/her experience, but often adds "EXCEPT FOR...." Because of these conversations, I found the friend's revelation about her father, "the only time / she ever heard her father talk about the war / he'd fought in years before in the Pacific" very credible, thus transitioning realistically to "Then he said nothing more." The poem ends powerfully. Not only does his silence reflect many military experiences that are kept unspoken, but his solitary silence at the end serves as an excellent parallel to the beginning lines of the group conversation.

Becky Faber
Lincoln, Nebraska

Cattywampus

The night is just a headless day.
    Footsore, it stumbles and stills,
        patient worm,
           lies glossed on rain water and
              sodium lamps.
The night has no socks.
    The night buries moons in dirty
        laundry, suffocates stars,
           which are only, we all know,
              the dead smoking in bed. A scream
           smokes around corners, a machine cries
        like a crime scene. It is not young,
the scream. It has more rust than
        the grinding gears, it is unlubricated
        by hope.
The dead have stolen the moon's shoes.
    Unclap the hands, unshine the diamonds
        of the unsung sun, brief hero. We, instead, worm
           into night, like lovers,
              like dog hair,
           like a disease. The sun, decapitated,
        rolls away into someone else's trash. The sun
stares unseeing at the place where
        the scream fell down. Disarticulated cops
           package it badly, ribbon it
              as their own. Chickens peck at radios.
        Smoking,
           smoking.
The scream is gifted elsewhere,
        eulogized on the patient pavement, old worm.
           The machine is too tired to
              heal itself, steadfastly marches
           into night, its chipped fans whining, the only
    hero of this story.

Laura Saint Martin
Rancho Cucamonga, California

About "Cattywampus":
A *Plainsongs* Award Poem

The title of this poem by Laura Saint Martin draws our attention to its shape as the lineation "stumbles" like the night and she describes a world in which all is askew, from the "sun, decapitated" to the "disarticulated cops" who handle it. From the assertive statements that begin at the left-hand margin, the poem unfolds into a series of interconnected images that become more elusive and surreal as we continue reading. The precision of the opening metaphor turns awry as the "headless" and "footsore" night becomes a worm in a reflective puddle. This placid worm reappears in the closing lines in an affectionate address but only after it has momentarily been transformed in a motion rather than an object as "We, instead, worm / into night."

    Punctuation and line breaks contribute to the deliberate and careful tone of "Cattywampus" as the difficulties of comprehensive description are overcome through Martin's repeated gifts of bizarre and yet utterly concrete images: after all, "we all know" that the stars are "the dead smoking in bed." The reader is co-opted into the poet's vision through this use of the plural first person as well as the present tense sustained throughout the poem. Our senses are fully engaged in trying to observe and inhabit the machinations of this fearsome creature: the "cattywampus" of night glimpsed as it "smokes around corners." I am reminded of T.S. Eliot's burn-out ends and cat-like fog as well as of W.B. Yeats's rough and slouching beast.

    Modern and prosaic realities such as "dirty laundry" and "dog hair" recur in a poem that concludes with the "whining … machine" as "the only / hero." However, Martin's mythic night also relies on continued rituals as the poet invokes its fall: "Unclap the hands, unshine the diamonds, / of the unsung sun, brief hero." The muse refuses to glory in the light and instead asks us to attend to the sinister delights of the dark.

Eleanor Reeds
Hastings, Nebraska

My Neighbor Henry

served as an army medic in Vietnam and the Gulf War.
He worked as an EMT for a while but his clarity quit.
He'd arrive on the scene and blink and then
find himself in the jungle or the desert
instead of an accident on I-65.

He sits on his stoop now, waiting
for his pension check so he can destroy
30-racks of Natural Ice and lottery tickets.
Back and forth, the trains go by.
Henry watches them, waiting
for one to stop right in front of him
and reveal the code on its broadside.
These are his lucky numbers.

He sits on his stoop now, tooting
along to jazz on his trombone.
Alexa, play Miles Davis, he shouts.
After more beers he plays Taps
with no accompaniment.

Every morning I wake up
to the angry blows
of a wooden two-by-four
crushing cans against
the concrete slab of his stoop.
Money from empty cans for full cans.

My father was an alcoholic, so I like Henry.
On the 4th of July I wanted
to bring him a 6er of Miller Lite,
drink it with him, thank him for his service.
I don't know why I didn't.

Sometimes I sit on my stoop, waiting
for what I don't know.
Back and forth, the trains go by.
I watch them, waiting

for one to stop right in front of me
and display the graffiti on its canvas.
This is my art gallery.

Sometimes Henry sees me,
walks over with a jar of moonshine.
Back and forth, the jar goes between us.
Back and forth, Henry and I talk
about football, about the weather,
about the neighbors who take days
to pull their bins up from the curb.

Then he returns to his stoop
and I return to my life.
Back and forth, the trains go by.

John Matthew Steinhafel
Bowling Green, Kentucky

About "My Neighbor Henry": A *Plainsongs* Award Poem

In John Michael Steinhafel's "My Neighbor Henry," the poet builds the narrative on imagery of Henry's history of being damaged and hobbled by war. The poem's tight focus details Henry's actions and his humanity, revealing the connection to the narrator. Its structure and repetition build a split screen of both Henry and the narrator.

Steinhafel's narrator is not aloof; in fact, the narrator adds touches of his own life, adding depth to his compassion. "Neighbor Henry" and the narrator are given equal space. The repeated use of the train cars helps achieve this:

> Back and forth, the trains go by.
> Henry watches them, waiting
> for one to stop right in front of him
> and reveal the code on its broadside.
> These are his lucky numbers.

Later, the narrator declares,

> Back and forth, the trains go by.
> I watch them, waiting
> for one to stop right in front of me
> and display the graffiti on its canvas.
> This is my art gallery.

Steinhafel creates the kinship of the two characters that provides the framework of the poem.

The poet works hard to show the connection between the narrator and Henry, to show empathy. While Henry wakes his neighbor by flattening beer cans with "angry blows," he reveals, "My father was an alcoholic, so I like Henry." There's enough complication in those insights to fuel a novel.

Steinhafel develops each character fully and brings the two men together: "Sometimes Henry sees me, / walks over with a jar of moonshine." As they sit on the stoop, the narrator adds, "the jar goes between us" and the two "talk about football, about the weather, about the neighbors."

By the end of the poem, the reader has traveled an amazing path, a human trail of how people endure and move along and get along.

And "Back and forth, the trains go by."

Michael Catherwood
Omaha, Nebraska

Persimmons

Punish the impatient
who attempt a heist of First Frost's Gift
    Greedy grandchild—
    Don't you know that bitter fruit awaits bitter weather?

Sit down, and I will tell you a story—
    It begins in bleak winter
    when under ice the crop matures
    look inside, the forecast inscribed in seeds

    Fruits who know the future—
    their divination done by Fork, Knife, and Spoon

It doesn't do to rush these things—
    A premature taste of prophecy will spoil your food
    Did you think you could have both?
    The comfort of summer and the snow's reward?

So until freezing glitter clings to the Earth
don't you go into that forest—
    seeking an Oracle Tree
    a fruit freckled goddess

who will pluck one of her berry earrings
    anointing your tongue
    for an ancient wintry ritual.

Jayne Macke
Imperial, Missouri

Seduction at the Oregon Coast Aquarium

Sex is not straightforward in the sea.
     Aquarium placard

On the concrete floor with tourists
smelling like shore life,
I stare into a round tank
as tall as the ceiling.

The glass magnifies
fourteen jellyfish:
Pink, protected, gauze-like,
undulant lace
in lucent saline,
they bulge and flatten
their way through the water.

Their tendrils mime
union, trail and trap food,
and in a silent chorus,
they pulse "come hither" to me
in the old slow motion
that makes me
catch my   catch my   breath.

I am saltwater.
You are moving
inside me now.

Shelley Reece
Portland, Oregon

Biopsy

Aspirate me
Pull this unholy stone
from my flesh, a gargoyle
in my temple, petrified
grimace open wide, spewing its heresy
into my aisles and side chapels

Crack my transept walls
pierce my dim nooks with a shaft
of daylight, dust motes radiant
round the monstrance on my altar
glinting against the red
vestments of my veins

Probe my habits
See if my pebbly breast
has embraced the enemy's creed
Elevate the devil's grail
secreted in my sanctum
and note if I genuflect

If I'm found impure, scour
my temple clean. Trundle
all the idols out of my chancel
and into the plaza
Stack the kindling high
It's time for a burning

Apply the torch
while I laugh
I've been skittished to a stake
for weeks, but the rope's loose
and the streets bounding the square
beckon me

Peter Snow
South Burlington, Vermont

He's losing words

They tumble from my keyboard.
Words, lines, paragraphs, pages.

Gifts for my friend's father. She said,
He's losing words.

He remembers the weather. He'll have a weather
for you, for you, for her and for him.

You're worried about your son's drinking habit.
He says, *There will be precipitations.*

For or against euthanasia, the tempers run high. He says,
Easterly winds of up to 80 km per hour expected.

Then he looks up, frightened.
Bites his cheek, asks his hands,

Where are my words? Checks his synapses,
looks at Prussian-blue horizons, cloud formations

bunching up across the contrails, pixellated,
somewhere beyond Orion.

Rose Mary Boehm
Lima, Peru

Cheerfully

Standing on the drowned shore
after another survival, we
know each other's first move
will be towards security,
shelter then water. Best to
take a breath and calm down.
We allow for each other.
You've always been impulsive,
the glad one, any wreckage
of the past shedding off your
child-swift soul as easily
as a casual young hero discards
her chicken-wire wings
at the call to supper.
You are the kite pulling
steadily upward against
my own caution-kinked ways.

Last ravens circle
in the evening dusk,
the attendant cloud
a smudged question mark
drifting away incarnadine.
We caused all that?

What fun uncertainty
has been with you. True,
this isn't exactly the gentle
retirement in a rocker we pictured,
but we *are* still laughing,
and there does at least
seem to be chocolate for
the wake of this apocalypse.

P M F Johnson
Minneapolis, Minnesota

Anemone

Just by saying the name,
For an instant, you become beautiful.
Some bigger sun blooms your eye with daydreams.
You see: wolves nuzzling wildflowers;
Scarlet windflowers on a windy hill;
Spring's rainy breezes tumbling green.
You find you're nothing like them,
Rooted in solitude among friends,
Ogling their stigma bulbs, dry for the blood
And nectar of heroes and goddesses
Long ago bulldozed and forgotten.
Your personality seems fake and rotten.
You tilt out of the sun, surprised
By how long it takes to find your phone.
Even after the first three texts
You feel clumsy and lightheaded.
Someone else drives while you fall
Into the flower of the mind
Dazzled by the possibility
Of bursting from your body
In a body of light.

Daniel E. Blackston
Springfield, Illinois

Houseflies

In all probability, houseflies possess
no metaphysics. Judging merely by

size, one would imagine they need
it more urgently than any of us. It is

life-threatening to be so small in a vast
vast universe. How they survive is

anyone's guess, but in all likelihood,
they must know a secret or two about

other worlds, the way they appear and
then disappear into thin air, just like that.

Faiz Ahmad
New Delhi, India

Hard Winter

The dogs met first
Sniffing and circling
then chasing and wrestling
as dogs will do when
housebound too long

We smiled indulgently at their antics
Congratulated each other for being
good owners in the bitter cold
Her daughter's dog she said

We noticed each other's accents
Wisconsin and Minnesota
She's been here 4 years now
What brought her to Nebraska I asked
To help my daughter with an illness
she answered
I hope she is better I offered
She died a year ago today she said

I moved to stand shoulder to shoulder
Hovered an arm behind her back
This is the coldest winter since
I moved here she said

I wanted to tell her we almost lost our younger daughter
but almost is not lost and doesn't count
That we mourned our older daughter's best friend
killed by a sun-blinded driver
But I couldn't connect that cataclysm of pain
with the interminable tides
of misplaced hope and despair she knew

We talked about our layers of clothes
Marveled how paws seem impervious
to below-zero weather
Her daughter's dog sleeps with her now
even though she lives with the grandkids

and son-in-law
Maybe he knows I need it she said
Dogs are smart we agreed

We talked about the new dog park
that neither of us has visited
I'm divorced now she said
I guess things like losing my daughter
are hard on a marriage
I've heard that happens I said

We stamped our boots on the frozen ground
Admitted our defeat
Exchanged first names
and handshakes
She set out for home with her daughter's dog
adrift and solitary across the snow
Borne on an iceberg of grief

Kathy Jacobs
Lincoln, Nebraska

A Tipsy Librarian

A wrinkled star at the hips,
the last place you will ever find her,
the sense enough of candied peanuts from a jar.

She adjusts her feet on elevated surfaces,
first a table then a counter top,
her right foot lifted, then the opening hinge
of pointed toes.

She is the drunken ballerina of this kitchen.
The empty set that holds algebra hostage.
I have seen her kind before,
the elderly neighbor says, devoid of kindness.

Autumn comes with its annual tradition of raking
books into discrete piles, a straddle of jeans
and the branch on the wall hand me my winter hat,
the difference between elk and elegant
misappropriated on the page like a brick wall
in defense of mortar: a picture hanging
in the hallway, a cicada stepping outside of itself,
leaving only the song inside.

Mickie Kennedy
Kingsville, Maryland

Some Winter

No one will die, be dying
    or even thinking about it.

        Friends will not mourn and sip
            cold coffee in church basements

but gather before warm fires to laugh
    and plan snow-filled adventures.

        Some winter the only angels, to speak of,
            will be those made in the snow by children.

Stars, silent and immutable,
    will keep their distance. And all

        my poems will be summer birds
            flying north to brave the winter.

Jane Costain
Denver, Colorado

The Itch

I used to imagine my own need
as an event horizon. Did you encourage that?
Beneath the surface of the earth, cicadas lay
frozen in wait; nitrogen moves
toward root interstates, and fungus communicates
danger between trees. I have no regret
about choosing my own happiness
and taking the easy path. It wasn't so
easy. I pulled thread from my body
and you never asked where the stitches were
and why. Things always end up
mended. This lack of curiosity
is a passive violence. You never want to look
at the floor of the forest. I turned my ear to the east.
I dug my fingers in the yellowing needles. I heard
the voice. I felt it: a million grubs
stirring in my own soil.

Emily Hockaday
Queens, New York

Living with Hawks

The red-tailed hawk
descends with intent
wings curled, legs thrust forward
then disappears
among blades of bluestem
dotted with blossoms
of spring spiderwort
wild bergamot and yarrow

A moment later it emerges—
squirming white-footed mouse
clasped in its talons—
flies to the low branch of a burr oak
and begins to tear and feed
skinning puffs of fur
dropping bits of bloody scraps
to the ground

But the sparrows still swoop
the chipmunks play
and a male sandhill crane
continues his courtship dance
hopping awkwardly for a female
with a blank stare
while perched doves mourn
and the cicadas thrum

on and on and on

Elisabeth Harrahy
Oconomowoc, Wisconsin

Hitchhiking at 19

meant getting picked up
by middle aged men
who never wanted anything
other than to know what my major in college
was and where I wanted to go
with that

until a balding creep one day
drove me into a parking lot at a cheap motel
and detailed how
he wanted it.

The word Motherfucker
came out of my mouth
a word I had never said before
leaving me speechless the long walk home
trying to picture what it was it would do to my mom
if he did me

and all Mom said when I walked in
right as she was serving dinner was *That was close*
in a tone I'd never heard before
that made me think
she was better than me at picturing—

Jo-Anne Cappeluti
Brea, California

Thoreau Reconsiders

In moments of despair,
Thoreau considered
the consolations of suicide

but there was no guarantee
that the other side would
offer the same grace of moonlight
against Walden's face,
or the wet smell of rotting leaves
plastered to roots and rocks
on Concord's paths,

or the nostrils' sense
for still-distant
snow—or the call of the
crow—or the west wind's song
in oak and maple tops
or the dawn's first scintilla
of sun dousing night's last
mourning star of regret.

Thoreau took comfort
in how none of these could
consider consolations
of other sides:
they were too busy

living on the only
side they knew.

Ken Craft
Wells, Maine

Orbit of Tongues

Sometimes we love in a vast terrain
foreign as the moon—made up even
by news footage, the travails of others,
virtual eyes, mouths, tongues.

It is Indian summer. We amble through
a meadow of spent lupine and hay,
eying each other as though to ask,
Can you hear me from this side of earth?

**Gwenn Nusbaum
New York, New York**

The Percipient

after Hardy

My friends speak of the dead
as if they were on vacation
or shopping in the city and
will be home before dark.

Not as if they have gone
where they were before they came
and now ride the orbiting earth,
lurk among the stars, and

mingle with iris and pansies
in the backyard bed, with
robins and redbirds breaking
the pre-dawn silence,

neighbors' dogs yapping
after alley walkers, greening
buds of crepe myrtle creeping
toward purple bloom. As if

they aren't always with us.

Harry Moore
Decatur, Alabama

Self-Portrait in Mixed Media

No starlight current rockets through my veins.
No. My blood is lava. There is plenty of time

to run. But the fire holds my gaze.
It looks careless to the observer. It is not.

Monstrous despondency and plaster.
A murder of crows. A trick of mirrors.

When you're looking at me, you're really looking
at you. It's better this way.

I keep my credit score low like my expectations.
My bikini line unkempt under my clothes.

My teeth polished and on display. But I don't pretend
to be so precious, or light as bird bones picked

clean and dropped. A hulk of mass to a small thing.

Trisha Daigle
Minneapolis, Minnesota

night ode

you, cold mouth
stretched wide,
stuffed promise
to hold our desires
for a later request

you, swinging
swallower,
bloom prolonger,
metal belly of kind
refusal to digest

you, night watch
of kitchen door,
sporadic cycler
of song hummed
softly into floor,
prerequisite
of our preservation,
rest.

Ali Beheler
Hastings, Nebraska

The Secret

A secret hides among
the bushes growing up
around my house,
lurking perhaps among
my tulip bulbs or daffodils,

a secret cuddling the roots
of shy white snowdrops, even
daring dandelions, muffling
sounds of burrowing owls
and moles and gophers—
oh, the list goes on—

as have the years—that taxi
driver stating to my friend
as they drove past, that he
despised my house, because
he lost his thumb here
while he was building it.

And so throughout the years
I've thought about his thumb,
that secret long asleep, hidden
lost and numb beneath
my irises and triliums.

Marilyn Dorf
Lincoln, Nebraska

Suicide Watch

When coyote comes toward you
confuse him by sniffing his ass.
    Norman Minnick

I followed the coyote from his poems
into mine, into woods, found him under

the last of autumn leaves in the trees.
The ridges peppered auburn and brown,

with winter in the late fall winds, clouds
went dark as if a dusk swept through.

I never knew him, but faculty who did
passed around a sheaf of his poems after

he hanged himself. I taught remedial
English at night too, same administration

closing their writing centers, insisting
pay would never improve, that even more

tenured faculty would be fired. Clouds
clear above us; I don't know what to say.

I can only offer him a goodbye, to mark
my own leaving, all of his goodbyes

behind him. Coyote beckons me to stay
with blue sky, an orange sun behind his

head like an icon. But I'm coming back
to try to finish this poem so I can bury it.

B.J. Wilson
Jacksonville, Alabama

High Wire Suite

Love is its own rescue; for we, at our supremist, are but its trembling emblems.
   Emily Dickinson, from a letter to Henry Wentworth Higginson, 1863

I.

What you think it is. It is not (lightness,
space). It is. Whoever. Everything.

To feel alive, does not need to be. Nor could
become
one.

As for this book—
it is useless.

II.

With your back on the wire: vastness,
the sky. Leave the have-been.

Step by step   to reach the world.
The earth itself

rests, is the path between
one star and the next.

III.

On one foot, on the other foot, again, and again, and again.

IV.

I present myself.
Grab hold.   Begin.

Give the only things
I ever remember.
The rest

does not belong to me.

Lee Peterson
State College, Pennsylvania

Note: "High Wire Suite" is composed of found text, from Phillippe Petit's "On the High Wire," trans. by Paul Auster.

social distancing

outside we stand a coffin length away
measuring the distance with our shadows

my neighbor paces back two sidewalk squares
and we talk across as if this game is hopscotch

or foursquare and death is a ball
that we try not to bounce to each other

or step on the cracks although these days a mother
with a broken back sounds like

a thing with an easy answer
a mimeographed worksheet of a problem

all purple and damp like these pansies
tipping their faces to the same

sky it's ever been all yellow and blue and white
a child's Easter basket of an afternoon

until another ambulance squeals by
and the grass bends over

winded

Doritt Carroll
Bethesda, Maryland

Midafternoon, December

Standing at the top of an extension ladder
just under the apex of the roof of his house
is an elderly man, the center branch
on this aluminum tree. His hair silver
in the snow-bright sun, hands
swaying as they twist and change
Christmas lights, bulbs brilliant as birds,
cardinal and jay. One at a time they perch.
An oriole flits to his left jacket pocket; its twin takes wing
from the right.

Sometimes he just cups them
in the wrinkled nest of his palms
and breathes and balances
and listens.

Lisa Roullard
Salt Lake City, Utah

Better Embers

Betelgeuse explodes on a Saturday after burning
through hydrogen, through helium, through silicon and carbon,
through any fuel it found fit for consumption.
Hungry inhabitants of many distant worlds
pause whatever they call foraging and reap
the supernova's plenty. Until it's not
a deviation from the permanent firmament
they thought they knew, they refuse the stew
just at a boil, the next definite meal.
By some unplanned agreement almost half
the puny fires normally revered are left
untended and extinguish gracelessly,
unseen by starstruck aliens who, even lacking
chin or wit, quit surviving and look up.

Thomas Mixon
Sunapee, New Hampshire

Midwest Crossing

That first long stretch we called Pennsylvania.
In a tourist shed we read the signs
that told where we could go if we had time.

Ohio is your least favorite state,
unless it's Indiana or Illinois.
I don't have one yet.

We bought our cheese in Wisconsin,
neglected it in the seat that sleepless night,
left it in an icebox in South Dakota.

Minnesota we fucked across, did all those things
eighteen-year-olds get killed doing.
We never got out of the car to do them.

How I fit in your lap—
How you steered with
the middle fingers of the left hand—

Border: solemn dawn.
We alone for gray miles in the middle
of millions of snakes of lightning aiming at us,

missing,
and you afraid—
a rare sight:

You Afraid.
I shall never see you
afraid again.

Kathryn Paulsen
New York, New York

Undone

I have never seen my mother naked.

But once I saw her
with her hair undone, the morning after
she found a photo of a woman with swollen nipples
in my father's suit jacket, and for some reason

it felt like the same kind of thing. Like her
signature French twist covered everything
natural about her and now she was just
flesh-skin, freckled
in the sun-stream pooling in our backyard.

It is a privilege to have
a beautiful mother. And everybody *thinks*
that their mother is beautiful, despite her bone-sharp
elbows and varicose veins, but none
of my friends' mothers were. Not like mine was.
Not particularly and I think we all noticed.
Their fathers must have too.

And I was there to see it. To see her,
alone and exposed beneath the curtain
of her own dark locks, bare feet
amongst the violets as she pinned
our summer clothes to the washline.

Her good cotton skirt.   My white-trimmed school socks.

Her deep purple blouse.

    My favorite shirt, with a butterfly on the front.

Yvonne Nguyen
Richmond, Virginia

Learning Long Division

Think back to a first cause, the void
that warmed the nest
of primary numbers, plumage blooming
from a zero's egg. Cheeks still flushed
by that furnace, we labored
in the bean fields of childhood,
were swept into the great mystery

of the teen love procession. We shotgunned
beginner beer on the steps of the neon
cathedral, its cross a flicker
among the pizza and fast
food signs. We cruised our Camaro
around the square, backseat lit up
like a Friday night stadium as a predestined

luster shone from our lips that lied
just enough to become a little
more than what we were—longing
to be what love wanted us to be—imaginary
numbers in this lethal abstract, impossible
remainders of an infinite
long division.

George Rawlins
San Diego, California

A Friend Tells Me an Anecdote about What It's Like to Be Black in America

an eccentric billionaire
kept tigers
dozens of these lonely
hunters, eyes on the throat
behind
white walls too high to scale

he was on his way to the university
routine turn
same street as yesterday
but void of life
the only other person
a police officer, his hand
already hovering at the holster
and advancing quickly
same street as yesterday
but void of witnesses

the moments that followed
how the heartbeat increases
until it flutters like a hummingbird
nears the speed of light
and makes the whole world pass in slow, slow motion
how you have time to think
but none to act
how a lifetime of fear
of this moment
pound your face against asphalt
an inch of metal piercing
holes through your lungs
the slow drowning sensation
and a moment of clarity
you have never owned your body

but this memory was not that

the eccentric billionaire
had released his tigers
sent them out to maul
and to be shot—
the police officer hurried my friend to safety

but he tells me,
that's being black
never knowing when you turn that street
if you'll meet
a man or a tiger

Michael DeMaranville
Taylorsville, Utah

Mermaids in the Basement

I started early—Took my Dog—
And visited the Sea—
The Mermaids in the Basement
Came out to look at me—
   Emily Dickinson (656)

We ride the silver-scaled escalator—
Mom, Aunt Alvina, my sister Nancy, me—
down to the depths of Sibley's, our premier
department store in Rochester. Sweltering air
assails us in this lush bargain paradise,

where lace pastel brassieres pile up like sand
dollars on the beach. Dim lighting
gives the mannequins an eerie underwater glow—
akin to mermaids without their sequin tails.
We swim around an island of frothy bathing suits.

Auntie vamps in a dressing room,
wagging her make-believe tail in the mirror.
A sales clerk with crustacean features
waves us toward sunglasses spying from a rack.
At the lunch counter we order hot dogs

slathered in mustard, yellow as neon surfboards.
Mothers guard toddlers bobbing in the aisles,
as time sails by. Sleepy after shopping,
we sift through our brightly-colored handbags—
and shell out cash before the tide comes in.

Shirley J. Brewer
Baltimore, Maryland

Mama's Suffering

For Mama, there's only matrimony and motherhood.
There's just Mama, never a girl, but a surrogate
for her brothers and sisters before Granny explains
the garden, a man's rib, the serpent, Eve's sin.
And there's just a boy, with his reddened hands
that never held anything long enough to love,
but he loves the comfort he finds in Mama's blue eyes,
the cool comfort after a summer rain.
There are no roses, no sweet nothings.
There is no string attaching rib to rib.
There's no sweeping Mama off her feet.
Mama and Daddy meet at Winn Dixie.
Mama bags groceries, Daddy cuts meat.

Brittany J. Barron
Tallahassee, Florida

Gutestellezumhalten...or is it *Zumhaltengezwungenerort*

There must be a word for it—
that place in a river, waterway, or gutter,
where the detritus washing downstream lodges,
where the river bends,
where the debris finds blockage
of downed tree, weeds in the pavement crack,
where the logs and leaves and bones and spiders
find their resting place.

I think I'll wake in the middle of the night and
remember the wayward word
for which I search, but I never do.
My memory is blocked by some protuberance
that grabs at the volume of knowledge
gathered by the stream of my years
collecting the combination of pearls
and putrescence that snags at that place
that defines the word I'm looking for.

I pick at my memory
like the tongue licks and flicks a loose tooth,
ignoring it, then returning to it
until the word *logjam* falls out,
but that is too narrow in meaning.

Perhaps there is no word to remember.
Maybe there's only a long German word unknown to me
that encompasses this philosophical idea:
an impasse that stops movement forward,
but also a place you know will provide stoppage
since it always has, the spot
where everything ends up, the place
in the gutter in front of my house where, this autumn,
all my neighbors' leaves will
stop blowing in the crisp winds and rest,
whether I have a word for it or not.

Renée Adams
Alexandria, Virginia

Digital Happy Hour

One thousand drinkers
dressed from the waist up in cocktail
finery—it is a fine thing

to quaff the strong stuff, to tear
a hole through the gauze of your
mask and make a little bird's nest
for a sipping straw,

to keep the blinds closed but still
open up a million pixel
windows, voyeur-venturing into
the living rooms filled with glass tables

picture frames on the wall, enclosing
school days and park walks,
the beach outings that left
backs a pink sandpaper
cracking like cooked lobster shells,

ignoring the fact that this was all once
a neon bath, and someone was in the back
singing about love while,
together, we envied that
immortal deer on the wall,

the one with his glazed, marble eyes
accepting our toasts while
a herd grazed in a meadow somewhere
saying, he was the one that
made it, that
survived. Everything.

Timothy McNeil Grant
San Francisco, California

This Is Not That Poem

The doyenne carefully creases the
origami paper, made of plant fibers,

mother sun and father rain. She folds
one memory against another and another

until, to her surprise, a shape comes out of
her hands that she has never seen in the

paper—a startled face, a silent mouth.
Perhaps this is not her life at all, perhaps it is

the paper seeking to express itself and the
shape it craves to assume no one has yet

been skilled enough to fold, just as though
the perfect poem has already been written

and it waits here in my pencil to be freed.

This is not that poem.

Tom Barlow
Columbus, Ohio

The River

And we went down
boys and girls together
in our school clothes
along the smelly creek
all the way to the river.
Brambles and stones
beneath our feet,
we passed rails and mill gates.
And there we stood
looking out in silence
at the great river
too wide to swim across
though some might have tried
and drowned too young.

And our teacher stepped in
allowing her skirt to rise
to her hips like a cloud
with her inside, and
lifting her arms she beckoned
one by one to her side
where she blessed aloud
our baptism, not to God,
but to the waters,
and we the fish
that lived inside
and it inside of us,
"Forever and forever,"
she simply said,
"You are one."
And some laughed for joy
and some bowed their heads
and cried.

Larry Smith
Huron, Ohio

Jackson County Pantoum

You tell me there ain't nothing there but home,
and I imagine that's just fine. The wind
plays out its autumn hymn through wheat
fields across the gypsum hills.

The wind is just fine, I imagine,
with quiet, clear sky and empty roads
that cut across the gypsum hills
like cirrus clouds through a sunset.

The quiet, clear, empty sky: a road
I could travel down as long as,
like cirrus cloud through a sunset,
it led to you in long cotton sleeves—

long as I could travel down—
like autumn wheat, a hymn playing
and you humming, the cotton fields in bloom—
ain't nothing there but home.
              So tell me.

Nolan Meditz
Weatherford, Oklahoma

Four Seasons

Fly in pirouettes
above the ice-scrimmed branches
of the sycamores that lift their arms
to tango with the winter moon.

Bloom like the first tulip
that drinks the April sun
as if it were a river of light
pouring into its open throat.

Hike the canyon floor
immersed in an ocean of silence
interrupted only by the flutter
of a butterfly's wings
flitting past your left ear.

Run ice cold water
over the ripe red apples
you picked this morning
from the tree in your backyard,
sweet and tart and unadorned.

Let no season leave you untouched
by the throbbing air
that signs its name in red on your cheeks,
be it the chill wind of winter
or the August sunburn
that peels away the layers
to the tender flesh beneath.

Gloria Heffernan
Syracuse, New York

meeresstille

the sea has never been calmer on the day we row
the glass-bottomed boat seven miles out to where the
seaweed floats free above the sand like an umbrella,

its arms pushed this way and that by currents we
cannot see. the sun beats down on the backs of our necks,
but we notice only its light, which pierces the water

at the same sharp angles as the rays which swim
beneath the boat as we draw away from shore.
the water has swept up a thousand miles of silver and silt

and dropped it in the open mouths of the corals here.
they drink oblivious to how the colours of the waves
shift as we pass over and the fish flit back and forth,

not confused, only curious. we lean over the sides
of the boat and take pictures even though we cannot
focus our cameras over the wavering sea. later,

we will lament how the fish are little more than blurs
in those pictures and how we failed to capture the stillness
in those split seconds of bliss before the storm.

Maggie Wang
Washington, D.C.

The Old Apple Tree

The title suggests this should be sentimental in tone
probably about how the children used to climb it and how

one of them sang her times tables from a high branch
or something about the pies or how two of our dogs

are buried beneath it or how a pair of downies have chiseled out
a nest in a dead branch or how it has lost big limbs recently

and that this spring the blossoms have appeared by the thousands
on its remaining branches a white and pink shroud that may

portend its breaking down a last fragrant show and how its fall
will be noted with a certain amount of mixed feelings

Mark Rhoads
Lino Lakes, Minnesota

Fishing for a Reader

I am fishing for a reader
who appreciates entanglement

and sees that the catfish and I
are reflections of each other

searching for something
we will not find tonight.

I am fishing for a reader
content to surrender

to a symphony of bullfrogs
cradled in constellations

stardust showering down
from worlds light years away.

**Ryan Nelson
Lincoln, Nebraska**

To the God Living in My Last Alveoli

Let my dry cough not interrupt my count
of the syllables and stresses along this line.
Let my music and meaning, together, mount
the infected air as a choking fire sign
as stone-black ravens, with death-filled ululations
circle around a mind-forged castle spire.
Its last pennant waves in my sputtering breath.
I won't stop here. I'm too tired to tire.
Despite retched-up brown blood coating my tongue,
with one hacked out phrase I add a parapet
where an imagined suicide had flung
himself to the sky. On seeing my last sunset
I search for words that could replicate the sun,
and hope my work would be our work when I'm done.

Marc Tretin
Valley Stream, New York

You Visit Me in a Dream at 3:36 AM

I didn't believe you
when you told me how frigid Iraq was—
the desert, your skin, and gunfire
always equated heat to me.
But here you are,
buzzed hair and a new tattoo,
your skin colored with the cold
and begging for warmth.

Polaroid, baby, purple, bacon, tune—
the words spill out fast.
Your lips are chapped and cracked.
Suddenly it is silent
because I tug you towards me and
your mouth tastes like decaying leaves
and maple syrup and broken pocket-watches.

Callie S. Blackstone
Connecticut

Face in Her Phone

An acrostic

White tails, ears perked, they stand watching
Her amble down a northern Minnesota road
In a hoodie up against the damp—she's unaware
Three does are a mere twenty feet away.
Engrossed in her walking head down,
They don't seem bothered or move to safety—
A thicket of shoulder-high brush nearby.
Instead they follow her with synchronized eyes,
Like supporting cast in a silent movie.
Dappled beside the curtained backdrop—
Elegantly choreographed, yet she misses this
Early morning wonder—lost to her own
Rambling texts about a meet-up at Starbucks.

Bonnie Larson Staiger
Bismarck, North Dakota

Open Casket

The corpse of a small bird
lies in front of our stoop;
each time we take a walk,
we take care to sidestep
it, past the white bones,
the exposed ribcage.

In Italy, there are so many bodies
that they cannot hold funerals.
Yet they still sing from balconies,
and I remember my mother,
as she wept for Christ, inside
Santa Maria Maggiore basilica,
golden with images of Mary,
the ceilings vaulted upward
to make us feel small, human.

Yesterday, we went to the park,
drank the sunshine, golden
on our faces. The birds, watching
us from the trees, still sang
from their perches. A moment
passed, and we forgot about
the bodies, let ourselves hold
hands, and closed our eyes.

Brittany Smart
Florence, Kentucky

Pink Plastic Caboodle

i never went to horse camp, or drowned
in coconut-vanilla glitter body spray

i always wanted to sell my soul
for a friendship bracelet

say an oath under the moon,
pale + lovely, cut my palm,

spill blood,
what's mine is yours:

strawberry lip balm,
our favorite horse,

was possessed,
our favorite horse was lucky
our favorite horse cried blood

crushes, sunscreen sack races,
bad cafeteria pizza
meant falling in lust,
scamming

potential lovers, pentagram scars
best friends forever.

Stephanie Valente
Brooklyn, New York

Spoken Over

You spoke over me for so long
that I fell asleep
in the valley of your mouth
and made a blanket from your tongue,
but even as I knit your taste buds
    into squares
and draped the finished quilt
    over my shoulder blades,
you didn't seem to notice
that I'd moved in.
So by the time you took a breath,
I had placed a tea table in the cavity
    of your left canine
and risen from my nap
to fashion a couch
from the soft cushioning
of your gums
    (which I'm pleased to report
    have not receded
    like your hairline)
and when you tried to speak again
    not long after,
you realized that your sound
was gone for good.
You had spoken over me
    for so long
that I'd grown comfortable
beneath your tongue,
rededicated your voice
to my own purposes,
and now you were forced to listen
    in silence
to the goings on of my day
as perhaps you should have done
    in the first place.

Emily Uduwana
Riverside, California

Because Memory Is Not Linear

Because the woman ahead of me on the path
lights a cigarette, because the menthol smoke

drifts back, wrapping me in a scent
of juniper and mint. Because thirty years ago

I sat in the backyard of Carole's duplex apartment,
a plot of grass around a cement stoop, a lit

Hibachi, Carole's children shrieking
at some game. Because in memory

Carole leans forward to light a Salem from a coal,
inhales like a practiced yogi, puffs out

the white smoke in fat O's. Because time
is not linear but pocked, moth-eaten

as old wool. Because time like memory
is a cold stream that swirls and abrades, that braids

the past into the future and the present
into past. Because anything I tell you

about Carole will be the Gospel truth.
Because what I leave out is just as true.

Because memory is green like hope or jealousy
or like Carole's green eyes. Because the woman

on the path ahead of me drops her cigarette
and crushes it under her heel. Because

Carole's children dance like memory
over the broken toys and scant grass. Because time

turns toward me again, opening her arms.

Bethany Reid
Edmonds, Washington

Silver Screen

A wintry matinee morning
and the front room picture window
has framed in the action outside so that
it looks like a black-and-white film.

The movie has something to do, it seems,
with snowflakes confetti-ing down
as cars and trucks alike shoulder into
an antagonistic north wind and

shivering rooftops wrap silvery stoles
about them to keep out the cold.
The plot is a study in contrast
that builds to a sparkling finale wherein

patches of ground, once dark and exposed,
don luminous ivory gowns,
each one as stunningly glamorous
as any that I've ever seen.

Michael Hill
Fort Collins, Colorado

It's Always within the Wood

He's sanding down
a branch he's taken
from under the trees
behind their house. He'll
sit here until noon, the air
taking the wood's slow dust.

In the afternoon, he'll take
his knife and start
to shave closer, circling
any knot, letting the grain
tell him where to go, letting
the shape arrive. Sometimes
a bird appears, sometimes
the moon, a boat, once
a hand, often only the smooth
world of curve and edge.
He knows when his hands say no.

Jack Ridl
Saugatuck, Michigan

Yes, No, Yes: An Acrostic

I exit from the Edens Expressway onto Fullerton, stoplight red at ramp bottom.

A homeless man spots my opening window as the Subaru rolls to a stop and he
Makes his way over, shuffling past puffs of exhaust visible in the winter air.

Need Money for Doctor reads the cardboard sign he carries in raw hands—
Only I reach into my glove compartment for a box of granola bars and
Thrust it toward him as the light turns green and he hurries forward. Just

Before I leave I see him look at the box, then at me, then at the box
Again. I turn left through the underpass and in my rearview mirror
Dozens of makeshift tents cluttering the dank space recede.

A flat note, a missed step, a blind eye, a loose grip.
My wheels are spinning.

I am freezing.

Amy Spungen
Highland Park, Illinois

The Scent of Rain

Researchers Discover Faraway Planet Where the Rain is Made of Iron.
  Huff Post, 3/11/2020

No rain can cool this new planet
scientists sighted in an iron cloud
400 light years away from Earth.
Twice as large as Jupiter, they say,
this foundry planet with no job openings.

On one side it's always day,
on the other night, one side is super-hot,
the other cooler at 1500 Celsius.
There the iron it's made of
rises as great clouds of Fe gas
that fall as rain. *A hard rain*
far beyond what Dylan sang—
heavy drops striking molten rock.
No quench possible from this
firestorm but blast and flare.
No life of any kind possible there.

How different I know the scent of rain
like the rusted pump handle at the old farm,
taste of water in the dented metal cup,
coolness on my hands that scooped
to splash my face hot summer days,
how the grass grew thick there under my feet.

Warm nights we slept on the porch
to better catch any breeze that passed,
listened for an owl's hoot, cicadas hum.
We huddled under cotton sheets
when wind blew the falling drops inside
as rain fell on the silvery metal roof.

Beth Paulson
Ouray, Colorado

Some Marriage Vows

One day you come to in
the bed and the flu has left you
and the hominoid days are over.
Your natural environment no longer
enfeebles you so much. Nary hangs a fret
over the service of emotional needs. True
love brings you a puppy.

This goes on until you realize that you
need a ghost (a realistic ghost who
knows how to play the bells and take
your hand absentmindedly or just
through the walls). There are no more
of the same challenges. Only Useful
Constraints—softest ropes and promises.

Yes. I will. I will live as long as I can,
with as much purpose as possibility
allows. I will make diagrams while our kids
are sick. I will cut out the rust. Make new
welds. Wax. Will serve. Flee from head on,

pitiful sadness. Listen. Follow. Are you excited
enough to keep going? I do vow to spin a mess
of clean electric and pleasure out of the air (night
or day or wet) and shamelessly knead it
into your ass/heart/neck (whenever you
so request). Until you no longer
need a companion.

William Greene
Sullivans Island, South Carolina

Perhaps Then

You are mouthfuls of rain and eyes of rolling thunder, snowcapped emotions and she-loves-me-not conundrums. And I am feverish remorse and avalanches of white flags turning red under sarsaparilla skies. I'd place dreams on the tails of comets and leave atmospheric burns across your skin if only we could travel to a time before the fireflies escaped and we trapped lightning in bottles. Perhaps then, you can suture the pieces of me that are no longer me and the fragments of you that separates our flesh from bone and love from lust and cauterize truth and hope back together. Perhaps then, we will collapse breathless and shaking, bare and breaking at Eros' altar and claim a heart that beats to the rhythm of forgotten fables. Perhaps then, with a steady hand and haunted heart I will chop love's martyrdom off at the knees so it can no longer run.

Stephanie Lamb
Casa Grande, Arizona

Ides of March

Rain returned overnight,
steady rattle on the skylights,
good for limp weeds
and canvas-back ducks
swimming in the bay,
but the mood indoors is gray,
edgy and between afternoon cloudbursts
I break outside, lurching
into the chilly air, find myself
on unpeopled streets, indulging
both freedom and safety, and except
for the sound of dripping trees
it's pretty quiet until I notice
the barely audible chirps of small birds,
brown-feathered with streaky whiteness
near the throat, and I look
more carefully as I pass
a grassy unoccupied playground,
spotting the first red robin pecking at mud,
hear the racket of ravens prowling
through wet garbage spilled
by the morning's recycling trucks,
a territory previously controlled
by blue jays but overtaken lately
by mobs of black birds
and realize I may be witnessing
another stage of evolutionary change,
these birds descendants of dinosaurs,
they know about extinction,
and with all this humming and whistling,
nibbling on willow buds and worms,
licking wet leaves, they're enjoying
the plight of their pedestrian rivals
who claim Biblical rights
to increase, multiply, replenish the earth,
unworried about global disaster,
and perhaps the birds
in their floozy mid-air exercises

expect to reclaim the power
and glory of the hero,
Tyrannosaurus Rex,
hoping to ride again, masters
of the universe, and what with rumors
of global warming, why not?

Peter Neil Carroll
Belmont, California

Indigo Barn on the Way to the Reading

On the way to Dhaka   On the way to lower Manhattan

Tell us their factory lives stitching   stacking   Triangle Shirtwaist
   Rana Plaza

Whose money is it heaps higher than mounds of cut bodices—
   bundles blocking doors—whose
piles of gold and paper bills soar past the sixth floor the eighth, stay
   neatly stacked while buildings burn and crumble?

Bucolic: is that the word for the landscape we are hurtling through?
   The women in the car on the
way to the reading—on the way to Dhaka on the way to lower
   Manhattan—are talking poetry and fries and the adjunct life and
   out the right-hand windows rising
above the dismal misplace of April snow

is the indigo barn. Some farmer was done with red, with *the way we
   do it.* Or was she done with
milking—tethered to the herd, sewed to stanchions morning,
   evening? Maybe another story: loving
most of the cows—these fields, that windbreak—but not the
   dwindling impossible price per gallon.

Who owns that labor, that product, whose is the creamery? Does
   she still call herself *farmer*, the one
who works retail in town now, who sold the house and the yard
and the barn to someone who basks in the quiet of a country life,
   sleeps in, can afford
to raise a few pullets, keep a horse, let the dogs run free, whose
   neighbor is not yet
a corporation?

Someone grows the only potatoes McDonald's will buy, sprays his
   fields from a concrete bunker.
Someone fills her bags with poems, one bag per class, teaches too
   many classes, pieces checks into a
rough collage of rent, milk, T-shirts.

Our shirts   Our glass of milk   The cream in our coffee   Our
   contracts   Our farm bill

Whose words? Whose banner of words flies in the hot wind over it
   all, in the blizzard? Tell us.

Suzanne Swanson
Saint Paul, Minnesota

The Sleeping Princess

(ATU 410)

1. A fairy casts a curse on a young princess.

With no spindles in the kingdom, production comes to a halt. The king's velvet cloak grows stiff and unsmooth. The queen's lace veil is dotted with pockmarks. The tailors tear the curtains from the princess' canopy to sew her ballroom gown.

2. The princess falls into a hundred-year sleep.

In her dream, she carries a spindle between her hands. She wanders through the woods as she works, spinning a long golden chain. For fear it will be lost, she uses a sailor's knot to anchor one end to her ankle.

3. A prince awakens her with a kiss.

She screams, but the rest of the kingdom has gone to sleep with her, and by the time anyone has risen, it is over.

She can no longer remember the dream, only fragments that occasionally light up in her mind like pebbles under the moonlight.

4. They are married that same day.

Afterwards, when the prince sleeps in their bed, the princess wanders the castle. Those who see her in her nightgown with her gray and brittle hair believe they have encountered a ghost.

In the mornings, these meetings go unmentioned.

Hailey Spencer
Seattle, Washington

Burn

This is only the very beginning
I am but flesh and bone
Papier-mâché and laced together
Gently
Like tears fall
Gently
Like worlds collapse

Lay me down
In rich black soil
Cover me with lilies
Sing a song for me
But only one
That when you hear it later
You may think of me
And the smell of soft, tilled earth

Survival is a compromise
Gray green and shifting
And this is only the very beginning

If you light me
I will burn
Remember this about me
If nothing else
I will burn

Ann Schlotzhauer
Overland Park, Kansas

How we remember and how we forget

In August when we walked after dinner
under summer constellations
out to the mailbox on the road
still radiant from the day's heat
I in a summer dress and he in shorts
we said Do you remember winter? Can you believe
we wore down jackets and hats
and boots with thick socks?

Those warm nights are unimaginable now.
Dropping thickly under the cold November rain
our crop of walnuts surprises us again—
the wet shells glow lava orange
where they fall on the gravel paths.
Bill straightens from picking them up
and complains It's so oppressive.
I remember how in July the farmer next door
genially cursed his peach harvest—peach hell
he called it and before that was apricot hell
and before that almond hell.

Our hands recount the week's work
with cuts and scrapes and dings
in May blisters from scythe and rake
in February small cracks from dry cold.
It's just the gouge of the day
the farmer next door says cheerfully
and following his example
we no longer bother with bandaids
but wrap our fingers with black electrical tape.
Somehow the skin closes over and we forget.

Susan Harvey
Vacaville, California

Breathe

Think ocean laps
Feel the sadness
On singed, hot thighs
Feel the particles of your skin on mine,
Of all the flag waving
Galas that your pie faced
Child self beamed at.

Breathe
The disappointment of the lost purse
The lips that brushed your lower
Temple
The tongue that lashed the lizard
Of your ear.
The prize lost in the sand
Under boardwalks
On dank city strips.

Breathe. Until you stop and join
The dead
Lilting on the ocean's lap
With no skin on any skin
Just cold, stretched canvas on
A drum.

Barbara Tramonte
Amherst, Massachusetts

Grappling with a Bit of Astrophysics and the Optimum Wrinkle Cream

What a piece of work is man
    William Shakespeare

It was for a time, a gnawing hunger,
to know for the sake of knowing
what was beyond the beyond,
what was inside every inside, how cats purr,
and if we are alone in the universe.

It was for the sheer joy of exploring
of the dog star and the red eye
of Jupiter with all those moons watching.
It was inventing compostable toilets.

It was, of course, time itself
and its avatar, space
It was a single molecule of helium,
and who makes the best chicken sandwich,
the god particle, and black holes

It was answers without questions and a bright
& carnal species constrained by gravity,
toying with nuclear physics, the optimum
wrinkle cream, interstellar travel.

Frank H. Coons
Denver, Colorado

Prelude to Pandemic

A cento

The news was an active volcano.
Something happened,
but nothing happened.

Inside the storm cloud, I watched
a baby falling out of a window
between the border of this

and the stigma of that.
What was more nuts was that
no one seemed to take note.

Forget the way men fall
down inside a lie—
the President has never

owned the rain.
How Satan must love to say
the name of God, must enjoy

holding aloft one middle finger.
How hard it has become to heal,
and to hold for your neighbor

the hysterical strength we must possess
to survive our very existence.
I turn on the kettle to make

my tea, hear the whistle start
to scream all those small terrors
you have to get up close to see.

Abby Caplin
San Francisco, California

Sources: [with lines taken from Valerie Bandura, Stephanie Burt, Kai Carlson-Wee, Chelsea Dingman, Jennifer Franklin, David Dodd Lee, Matthew Lippman, Alexis Orgera, Nicole Sealey, and Adam Scheffler on Love's Executive Order.]

Dear God of Condiments.

Why are you the only God in my refrigerator? Have I angered the God of Actual Food? My fridge is a shrine to you. Mayonnaise, salad dressing, mustard. Oh. How you gloriously and generously bestow your blessings upon me. You certainly taste better than a gun barrel.

Dear God of Condiments.

Have you ever tried making a mayonnaise soup? It tastes nothing like chowder no matter how much relish I put in. Have you ever tasted yourself, Dear God of Condiments? I confess, there have been times when I have licked my own skin, considered how well I could spread myself. I could compliment a corned beef and rye. I could be a sauerkraut. I'm told I am part German, but I don't know which part. I like to think it's my right pinky, shorter than my left. I am also told that I am a liar. If I said so myself who would believe me?

Dear God of Condiments.

It's not that I can't afford food, it's just that sometimes when I think about leaving my apartment I lose my appetite. I am sorry to say that I am not praying to you out of fear or admiration. At this point I pray to you out of necessity.

I am staring out of the window now. My neighbors don't know that I exist. In the Bible, they said that God spoke us into existence. I believe in a lot of gods, such as you, God of Condiments, as my fridge will testify. Little idols in the door defining my life. They say you are what you eat. Well. Here I am: two bottles of ketchup, a bear of honey, a jar of salsa, prostrating before you. Amen.

Gray Thomas
Salt Lake City, Utah

Hegel's Head

Sometimes, what you say and what you feel make no real sense

(Hegel's head)

A bell lies beside you in your bed

And you awaken engulfed. No shape before your eyes
only a sigh and a voice like the poet Christopher Smart
who wrote "Jubilate Agno"
while manic and in an asylum.

For the instruments are by their rhimes
For the cymbal rhimes are bell…

Soft vowels in your head. You must breathe into a bag

So, you get up and go for a walk with Christopher
Smart. Wandering and red, your eyes are breaches of
immanence.

There really are bells up there. And you are talking to
Christopher Smart, who might not be here.

And now you come to the silver bell inside its small
white tower, which sits beside the church where you
grew up. You pull the chain.

How sweet the sound
The bell calls
Soft vowels
Moist moon, morning-night
Rising sounds
Ringing along
the subtle change
in ring, rang, rung.

Bruce Alford
Baton Rouge, Louisiana

Anatomous

If you should rebuild me can you fill me up
out of a river and replace this slow blood
wandering around lost inside of me,
maybe looking for a heart,

install roll-down windows instead of eyes
that will watch instead of observe, squint
instead of judge and let in just a little
of that cool breeze I never see anyway

and maybe you have something to replace these
old hired hands I tried to give up to the bosses,
just like they tell you, sacrifice your hands
but keep the soul, but they wanted all my parts

and speaking of souls, have we decided if
they exist? I was going to ask for one
of those too, but it doesn't seem to go that
well with the world I've been wearing lately.

Casey Killingsworth
Stevenson, Washington

Rose in a Blue Vase

in memory of Gloria

Dry as old
toast, petals

transmute red
to beige; curl

like ribbon-
candy on

marbled plates
in the grand

old parlors
of long ago.

Rose, in a blue
vase, lamplit.

Kathleen McCann
North Weymouth, Massachusetts

Include Everyone

The next ark will have to be bigger.
Two by two won't be enough. The
Numbers have grown and multiplied.
Take the eggplants, the loblolly pines,
The cardinals, the rabbit, the crows.
The honeysuckle vines. Azaleas,
Tomatoes, and books. A chair.
A creek. Fishing pole. Hooks.
Tulip poplar, marigold. Honey,
Cherry, rose. Hydrangea and grass.
The skink, the anole, butterfly, moth.
Geranium, green pepper, begonia.
Pomegranate, sage, lavender and
Apple tree. Wasps. Bees. Palmetto.
Crepe myrtle. Rose of Sharon. Finch.
The sweet smelling mint. Gardenia in
Bloom. And this is just what lives
In your yard. You will need so much room.
Imagine the size of that ark. You better
Start building. It will be a long time
Before you are done. Include everyone.

Cassie Premo Steele
Columbia, South Carolina

The Streetsweeper

A streetsweeper lifts its glass
box onto Birch Circle. Its twin
moustaches spinning in curb silt.
Theodore's obsession with board
book representations of auto
mechanical monsters notwithstanding,
he cleaves to Lili's leg now
retreating from the foot of the driveway.

How many times have I tuned in
to the static of rain without wondering
what channel I'm on, what might
be waiting on the other side of the screen.
Through the bay window, I catch
glimpses of the long-haired woman
I married. Her dark shape flitting
around in the kitchen appears
intermittently crossing Venetian blinds,
L.E.D. strips of tacked below the cabinets.

I will never fully know my wife,
her triggers, her backstory the light
that nimbuses her tantrums, her paroxysms
of rage. Something lurks in her.
After our son brought down the shower
curtain, I discovered his terror
of forklifts at Home Depot. Just the two
of us in search of the elusive
rod, a lost shopping cart trundling
in the endless aisles of what it means
to be a man, what it means
to make things right.

Cameron Morse
Blue Springs, Missouri

Core

for C.B. & D.B.

Nothing nearly so large, unearthly
pressure, molten iron, the planet's heart
ponderous in its turning, 50,000 years
for the magnetic needle to swing
from north to south; beneath
our shifting feet a firmament;

nor nearly so small, pink filaments
shape of the needle's hollow,
eighteen in all the surgeon extracts
from you, my love; a few days' waiting
for the earth to shift beneath our feet,
the black door of *what comes next* to open.

Geomagnetic; tectonic; some words are content
to sleep between the pages, to rise only
when called, but other words insist, grab you
by the neck and shake: *malignant; invasive.*
Might there be another core? Small, some say,
yet larger than this planetary tremor?

I find it with my hand touching your shoulder
when we walk through that door together.

Bill Griffin
Elkin, North Carolina

Letter to an Imaginary Friend

Dear Sassy,
Our garden is full of the husks
Of childhood fruit, ungoverned by family
Memories swirl, memory-ash
Sifted through the grate and
I missed the last murmur
Of the fire collapsing into itself
And I find myself at the gate-
House of an imaginary friend
The structure has fallen empty
Not even familiar in the crisp leaves
You and I sat on that old fig tree's
sideways branches, an easy climb
Or lay on the unmown grass
Gorging on figs, and small bitter
Apples, and the day closed, a fist
Around our trusting throats but once
Your house was real as the one
I must return to—you never own a house
The way you do that first house
Even if it was pretend all along
Even if you never owned a thing
But maybe I'll come again, Sassy
If you're home, maybe, we can talk

Saramanda Swigart
San Francisco, California

Blue Crayon

A blue crayon slips its case,
rolls randomly across
yesterday's nursery rhymes,
disappearing over the edge
of a kiddie-size preschool desk
to escape the sticky-fingered
daycare popup picture book rut,

and colors its way out
beyond the lines, zigzagging
in a quest to explore
unimaginable
boundaries elsewhere,

indulging itself to write
its new name, Cyan,
large in shaky letters,
as if guided by a child
unversed in penmanship,
seeking its likeness in kind,
drawing distinctions:

an editor's pencil, well used,
pointless, faintly chewed,
recalling a dull, distant cousin;

eyes infinitely deep
with possibilities
looking up, blinking uncertainty;

van Gogh's mad strokes of ennui,
crossing bridges at Arles
with rhythmic improvisation;

dark riffs howlin' down muddy
backstreets, callin' for a sign—
"Sweet Delta demons gonna sa-ave my soul";

and that circle of horizon
where sky greets ocean dazzled
in sunbeams—feeling not blue,
not Cyan, but Azure.

Richard T. Rauch
Lacombe, Louisiana

Muddy Water

The Red River churns in turbid circles
beneath the railroad bridge
in Winnipeg, once the murder capital
of the country, but not currently.
They've got ballet and the Museum
for Human Rights, I'm all for that,
and down by The Forks
there's an early spring fragrance
of tallgrass prairie and snowmelt.
Inveterate flâneur, I'm at home everywhere,
and here too, with my people,
the French and the Scottish,
the Chinese, the Métis, the Cree.

Ruth Holzer
Herndon, Virginia

Another Poem about Birds and Windows

a poem is like a window
in that it lets in light
where before light did not come
and in that you can hit your head on it
if you forget it's there
especially if you are a bird
and if you are a bird
you are already a poet
and if a bird hits your window
you become a poet, irrevocably
it is a law of physics
a by-law actually
established by poetry
under the aegis of physics
with which it coexists uncomfortably
because physics is all about
how when you throw something
you know what it's going to do
and poetry is throwing something
and having absolutely no idea
where it will land
or with what force
the bird has some idea, of course
that is why it weaves and lifts
to pass between the strands
of physics and poetry
both of which it is
cursed to comprehend
cursed to master flight
no less than faith
in the window's telling
and its skull so small
and its skull so certain in its arc

Katie Tunning
Jamaica Plain, Massachusetts

Dead Poets Society

On watching Dead Poets Society *in sophomore English five weeks after trying to kill myself*

I see what Neil is doing
before any other student.

I know he will be dead
before he puts on his crown
or opens the window
or closes his eyes.

A chorus of teenage laughter
rings into the hallway
as the screen's gunshot
echoes.

It was his ritual, explains my teacher
who will never be John Keating.

I wonder if they laughed
at my own empty
desk for two weeks.

None of them know
what it is like
to hold death
in their fingertips

or to let it go.

Jade Driscoll
Mount Pleasant, Michigan

Gonna Tell My Kids

That this is snow, pointing at ice I crushed from the freezer.
Adopt a fluffy white dog. We own the only polar bear.

The last riverbank in existence is Daytona Beach,
tubing is just connecting empty water bottles together that wash
    ashore.

Wintertime is for beach bodies, take selfies in front of castles
made of cremated rainforests and hardened magma.

The storms raging outside aren't like the ones back in my day.
They won't believe Memory #4, the one where we used to

play in the rain without radioactive droplets burning our skin,
singing as we caught them in our mouths. Hopping in puddles,
choreographed to jump as high as the dreams we were encouraged
to make before we graduated. The Real World™ handed us diplomas

with puppet strings attached. Master's degree Marionettes for $10
an hour, healthcare unnecessary for unreal boys and girls.

This is what I whisper to my abdomen. Explain why they cannot
    live
outside where Grandma and Grandpa beg them to be every day.

Gretchen Gales
Richmond, Virginia

Earth Wrapped Wood

Perhaps it's time to walk the mirror's bleak length,
to take the gorgon body as my own
to be wrapped in water's threading moonlit loam
and to give, to glance the gut that leaks not thanks,

not home. Instead, the hand a garnet error
as the coffin slips through soil worm-worn slits
and I fail my flesh the grasp of wooden plinth
as it carries my heart to maggots and horror-stone.

Are lilies leaning over black-mawed waters?
Are the rampant grief-full figures gone? Chagrin
gnaws her yellow teeth-like-tomes and lets in
the mourners to their greed and thieving haunts.

Here is the wild sour guilt that comes
the unboned weightless organ, my own, my home.

Haley Wooning
Vacaville, California

Unencumbered

This is how you get rid of it:
hold it loose, fingers curled around
like a cigarette kept dry in a
downpour. Walk quickly, with purpose.
You have a destination, whether you
realize it or not.

Once you have dropped it in the gutter
or a bin or beneath a bush, your speed
will increase, your gait relax, you'll be
a large cat galloping through badlands
that no longer intimidate.
Your movement will be easy and free.

Robert L. Penick
Louisville, Kentucky

Marx and Bakunin

If we set our sights early on Bakunin could
But wonder at Marx it wasn't we did
See only the disconnects also the profound
Affinities then we were t-shirt *Dead Kennedys* teens still don't
Knock that youth sees through every nearly
Platonic shadow presenting as the real deal til then
Again later in our 20s studying political philosophy when
We sure saw a different side of both the awkward theory
Too not just the edgy October actions it wasn't until
Maybe in our 30s and 40s that the two came back together finally

Into one Leftism. That's when we started rioting angry once
More this time with our younger kids even more angry than
We are. We shouted the two names—GEORGE FLOYD!—
All together we cried tears we
Fell in love and added life-changing fear.
This had become a war.

Jones Irwin
Dublin, Ireland

With My Mother on the Patio

Seems I've never noticed the morning sun
gauzy across her face, a silvered auburn
at her temples like the high fringe of trees

in the moment after sunrise,
the underside of a chickadee's wing
or its thin fluting trill,

albeit I'd never mistake her for a chickadee,
the mother I know is a blue jay
nested in the large cedar below the house,

in summer, the adult jays plummeting themselves
from its frilled upper branches, the entire bird
fixed into a passerine bayonet

sweeping whichever neighborhood cat
trespassed their tree. The other day
while caught in the strange

meanderings of memory,
watching a small cobalt bird
as it carried full beaks of lawn clippings

to the canopy of a nearby locust, I thought
of the double-murder up the road from my parents
in '05, though not of the gunshot echo

against the valley or the woman
bleeding to death in her front ditch
and the purebred dogs executed in their kennels,

I was thinking of my mother on the porch, stationed
with her father's rifle, round chambered, daring
any predator to emerge from the darkness.

Jae Dyche
Linden, Virginia

We Need Your Help

You don't know me but you'd like
to get to know me, right? I avoid
your gaze by trying to send a text,
but I can't connect from here. A television
blares from behind the bar. It's the ad
with the abused animals. Again. They
need my help! For the price of a cup
of coffee a day, I can make a difference.
I avert my eyes, but the song continues
until the bartender changes the channel,
saying, That's bringing me down, man,
to no one in particular. I notice you've
left but it doesn't matter. Someone else
will take your place in no time.

Michelle Brooks
Albuquerque, New Mexico

Cheesecake Monument

I've spent most of my life not fitting
Too rough
Too physical
Too fast
Too loud
Too dirty
I remember my Mom apologizing for me at some music lesson
I was dusty from the playground
I remember her being embarrassed
I embarrassed her

Too difficult for 1st communion and cheesecake
Hike up that white dress
It was itchy and uncomfortable and awkward and that made it even
    worse
I can still hear it
Come on, hike up that white dress, just a little cheesecake
How horrible
I was 7

Don't kill the grass under the tree
It's the only tree
So don't climb
Don't get dirty
Quit yelling
Ladies don't yell
Be a lady
Just a little cheesecake

The pictures are still up
Me yelling when I was 5
The cheesecake picture
Me memorialized as difficult
It's laughed at, a joke
A monument to my bad behavior

Kelly Hegi
Fridley, Minnesota

Downhill

the tongue clicks fast like a snake tasting air   chasing

pouring ink & bile down thoroughfares laid
    by strangers but filled
with particles of poison
    and sloshing saliva margaritas   salty sour

intoxicatingly pure in veins of promising platforms or
Serve and Protect

emptiness birthing confidence through   ignorance

mirages of honesty rippling   air

Stephen Ground
Winnipeg, Manitoba, Canada

Every Body Lies

That's what it says on her black tee-shirt,
the neighborhood girl's, in long white letters

stretched tight across her chest. And not
in two words—not "Everybody Lies," but

Every—Body—Lies.   We know a body
of evidence can jail the innocent man,

and still, we like to pretend: the wide body
of the plane pushes back from the gate

with the promise of safe arrival, the Atlantic
will forever belch out fish.   Every body lies.

The body of my ex, the one I knew best,
had lips that said he'd never leave

and legs that sped him out the door. Even my body,
my own, told me for the longest time

I wanted him to stay.

AE Hines
Portland, Oregon

Preparing for Our Past

This week I'm transplanting 20 trees and excavating mounds of
    porcelain. Which is to say, I'm
downhill ignoring someone who needs me. Or, I'm downhill
    supplanting my fragile needs with
chipped teacups.

Which is to say, someone and something came before me and
    dumped hard work down this hill.
Someone gave up and didn't rebuild. Someone took off with a
    parched throat and a lighter load.
Someone left me to clean up.

Maybe I'm too late for someone. Someone didn't know I'd
    eventually show. Sometimes we miss
our saviors by minutes. Saddled with tools and music from another
    time, sometimes we discover
we've been born too late.

•

Today my neighbor unearthed 200 shoes. Someone didn't know
    verity would sift through the
Vesuvius of their old soles. Maybe someone didn't know their
    honest work was built to last.

My neighbor and I drove 2000 odd miles on different days to plant
    ourselves on these hills. We
unshouldered our tools and took to foundations. Perched on low-
    profiles, we trusted in bright
horizons.

We dug earth for ochres to make signs for our futures. We found
    someone born sooner had
planted what we needed. Shoes to flee fires that are always drawing
    nearer and teacups to carry
our paints when we leave.

•

Which is to say, let's kick this can of the precious and poetic.
    Someday we'll rot, leaving all our
trash behind. Which is to say, despite all that we've cobbled
    together, we're nothing more than
the teacups we've tossed and the trees that we've planted.

Bradley David
Los Angeles, California

After…

First things first:
Tiptoe straight upstairs
so no one hears.

Then, keeping off the bathroom light,
quickly shuck the clothes
he said looked too sexy
for him to resist reacting to—
remember, don't glance into the mirror,
for you won't want to see what you would—
and stuff those offending
garments into a spare garbage bag
so you never need touch them again.

Turn the shower water to hot,
to a temperature as scalding as you can stand,
and beyond it, to a temperature that hurts
like the self-mortification of a holy woman
punishing herself because of her base human nature;
but nothing about you is holy now—
base, yes; holy, no—
since you finally stopped fighting and relented,
so that the surrender (although maybe lifesaving)
seems a mark of guilt you need to expunge as much as
the memory of his flesh, unwelcome, invading yours.

Shampoo in hair,
soap sliding over torso and limbs,
scrub hard
until bubbles erupt all over your body,
almost as dramatic as it appears in the ads,
except there's nothing elegant about this;
this, instead, is a desperate attempt to
wash off all trace of him, to
sterilize the skin he tainted, to
flush his filth down the drain, far, far away from here.

Margaret Adams Birth
Queens, New York

She wears a larch collar

after sugar toast and licking her fingers clean—
    like a billy goat—she giggles about the rough

and warm suckling—the teeth begging and the
    tongue begging and—the needing of her and

her needing every night at bedtime—a glass of
    water and her alarm clock set to get up alone—

leaning back in the center of the mattress—resting
    her head in the center of the pillow she pulls

the covers to her neck like a larch collar—she begins
    feeling for the wool—counting sheep—her body

changes: her knees: burls and her knuckles: knots
    and the immobility allows her—forces her—

to know what it means to inhale and exhale—to be
    woman and wife—daughter and mother—her fingers

are sticky and smell like billy goats—nudging her asleep—

Ed Sage
Portland, Oregon

Encounters with Strangers II

I find peace
off Main St. w/ the yarn shop
and the Alano Club rests
      the world's smallest cafe
Inside baristas are sitting on the floor,
flipping each other off talking
      How they'd like to disappear,
leave for France and only tell each other
In the kitchen, Bruce
      is chefing up something sinister
He poaches eggs like surgery
& when customers taste his pastries,
      behind his toys for eyeballs he asks
How well he did,
      If it was to my liking,
How slowly things move here
      Across the street middle aged men
purchase grain and dog food
      & their wives nextdoor
sneeze allergy and get their hair cut
      If you asked me
if I liked being at home I think I'd have to
        Lie either way
In the wintertime it gets so dark
      If I could tell you everything
I've wanted to do after sunset
      you'd think I'm crazy
        To kill time
we push shopping carts into themselves,
press each basket forward
      until a train forms
      Contest: who can control
the longest chain
      Such terrible sounds pass in the
Dark traffic sometimes rips
      the air we share
It's invasive, quite honestly
      how we look through each other's car windows

Desperate to catch a glance
    We see each other across a lane.

Joseph Felkers
Caledonia, Michigan

comfort

a phone call from Grandma
hardly words by now
just pictures
echoes
north of here
midwest of everywhere else
something about
corners
and the way streets match like dominoes
how passing corn fields flash rows
at speeding cars
only one green guarded hall visible at a time
something about
poor man's steak
and soup from a can
something about how every
man with a pen who has tried to
draw out what home is
has always
starved for ink
she doesn't know by now
that i've tied a rope from my house
to rainier
and every day i balance
wondering on which side i'll fall
love you much
is how we end
and we mean it

Benjamin Mast
Seattle, Washington

Chokecherry

Say something
just because it feels good
in your mouth.

Like the way
harpoon flows from the back
of the throat and then out like

a harpoon, like a gamma-ray burst
across a galaxy.

In Montana, flat land and
Mormons.

But not as many as Utah.

This is how we will speak of this:

A man with a stalk of grass
in his teeth, twirling and tasting
the way his drawl
tumbles through *entropy*.

A brow furrows. The Earth bulges
along her axis. Somewhere, a cow
steps on a twig, breaks
the tension.

I've driven through Montana, never
Utah. But I can imagine a weight to the air
from which even light
cannot escape.

Austin Veldman
South Bend, Indiana

Sassafras Tree in Snow

Stripped to bare essentials
        as the first flakes fall, the sassafras tree
in my backyard (next to the muddy drive I
        want to re-gravel, but worry I have no money
for that) shivers in the wind.

        Usually, I say, *Look, children, at that pretty
green tree.* Not knowing an oak from a locust,
a hickory from a maple.
        But as I learn to pay attention, I know more.

I know the sycamore, its flaking white bark—
        it reminds me of long summer days cutting
my grandmother's lawn. *Other Mama,*
        we called her. The tall tree out back of her house
        lost its bark in great strips—
I would tear through them with the mower,
        listening to *Summer's Cauldron.*

I know the tulip poplar, tall and straight with its
        tiny swords for elven warriors. And I know
the red oak and the sugar maple.
        I am learning other oaks and maples.
The locust still eludes me, but I see it more and more.

Cutting cedar trees for posts with a friend,
        I learn the hickory. *The hickory branches grow
straight from the trunk. This isn't a pignut. They make
        drumsticks from these. It's the one tree I could make money
        on when I was in the milling business.*
        Hickory is a humble tree that makes useful things.

Summertime on the Rockfish River, I find sheets of sycamore bark
        and use them as stationery for letters or love poems.
        I send them to no one in particular, and no one loves this
        about me,
        opening envelopes to find shredded pieces of bark
        inside.

>   The giant elm tree in the backyard survived the derecho
> and other storms. The barred owls sing in its limbs.
> The tree has grown around the wire from an old fence
> > and the chickens at times rest in its shade. Autumn, its
> > > leaves
> > > > blanket the ground below, then the wind blows
> > them into the woods.
>
> But today the sassafras bears my heart. In spring, its mitten
> > leaves look ready for winter, the season when it sheds
> > those leaves—stripping back to the essentials, ready for snow.
>
> And what do I know about the sassafras and love?
> > Not a thing, not a thing. In winter, uncloaked of all its leaves,
> > > the sassafras is my teacher. I wait to understand what it
> > > > says.
> > *Wait*, it says. *Be patient. Wait in the cold winter wind.*
> *Spring is coming. Spring is coming. Just you wait. Just you wait.*

Stuart Gunter
Schuyler, Virginia

Trust your instincts.

Subscribe to *Plainsongs*.

Please visit our website at corpuscallosumpress.com/plainsongs to subscribe via credit/debit card, PayPal, or check.

Our 2021 rates:
- One-year e-subscription ($10)
- One-year print subscription ($25)
- One-year print + e-subscription ($30)

Questions? Contact the editor at etucker@corpuscallosumpress.com or write to us:

      Corpus Callosum Press
      PO Box 1563
      Hastings, NE 68902

www.ingramcontent.com/pod-product-compliance
Lightning Source LLC
Chambersburg PA
CBHW070433010526
44118CB00014B/2030